# DIALECTICAL BEHAVIOR THERAPY

**Progress in Just 10 Days.**

**Rebalance Your Life**

.

Daniel Mason

# Table of Contents

# CHAPTER 1:
# DIALECTICAL BEHAVIOR THERAPY AND BPD

Dialectical Behavior Therapy (DBT) is one of a few cognitive therapies considered to be of use to people with BPD. DBT is not a therapy to "avoid trying to kill yourself;" instead, it involves helping people to develop lives worth sticking to for. Those goals (to have a life worth living and to stop suicidal behavior) go hand in hand, of course. Living is hard to want if your life isn't worth living, and if you're trying to end it, it's hard to develop a life worth living. Being suicidal is much like being locked up in a dark room — a room that is so dark you can't even see the doors to get out. In reality, the place has several doors; you just can't see them. One entry, however, has a faint light below it. This door is the "suicide door." It's very enticing the suicide door — it's easier to see than the other entries, and you just happen to have the key to it. So, you spend your time camping out at the door of suicide, sometimes just watching it and feeling comforted by the fact that there is a way out. You could open the door (that is, you might try suicide). The problem is that you cannot see the other entries that lead out of the darkroom and into a life worth living while you hang out at the suicide entrance. Walking through the suicide door is another problem: you have no idea what's behind it. Moving through that door is like walking into a pool when you don't know if it is full of water or bone-dry concrete. Who knows what to expect when you step through that door!

We don't know what happens to those people who kill themselves. Some people think that suicide offers peace or a way out of their problems, but what if that isn't true? Taking that is a pretty big risk. What if you killed yourself because your partner rejected you, only to find out that you are now condemned to an eternity of your partner being rejected again and again? Then you would be in great trouble, for you couldn't kill yourself to get out of being dead! DBT aims to help people with BPD find the other doors out of the darkroom and into the light of a life that is fulfilling, enjoyable, rewarding, and, above all, worth living.

## The Theory Behind DBT: Biosocial Theory

Most treatments are based on some sort of theory about what is causing the problems of the client. The treatment is based on theory. It explains why there are some problems and points therapists and clients in the direction of how to solve those problems. In DBT, this theory is called the theory of biosocialism or the biosocial theory. BPD is triggered by both biological factors (being born, especially emotionally unstable and intense), and social or environmental factors, according to the biosocial theory. Environment Invalidation According to the biosocial theory, people with BPD, are not only emotionally vulnerable but also grow up in environments where they never learn how to deal with their emotions. Remember, people don't help you learn to deal with your emotions in an invalidating environment. Instead, they might tell you that you are wrong to feel your emotions, or when you become emotional, they might punish or ignore you. Now, people aren't always saying these things in words; their actions sometimes communicate invalidation. Imagine you're on the bus, and a very heavy person steps on your foot and sits there; you're saying, "That really hurts," and he's saying, "Yeah, I can see that," but he's not shifting his foot. That is what happens in the invalidating setting often. Someone does something that annoys you, you say something about it, but he or she continues to do it. These are all examples of people not taking your emotions to heart in the environment. Additionally, even growing up in a family where everyone is different from you can be invalidating as before. Even if no one tells you something is wrong with you, you might think something is wrong with you — like you're the "black sheep" or an outsider. It can be really painful to think that you are different or more sensitive than others, or that you have a more difficult time to cope with your emotions. Finally, people with BPD often have a physical, emotional, and sexual history of abuse. These may also be considered parts of a disabling environment, but it is important to note that even if you have not been abused, you may still have experienced invalidation from caregivers or others around you.

People with BPD have had many of these experiences as they grew up, according to the biosocial theory. If you have BPD, you may also have had the experience of people avoiding you, getting angry with you, dismissing you, or refusing you when you've become particularly emotional. As a consequence, you might actually have started to fear your own emotions. Keep in mind, however, that what contributes to BPD is the combination of susceptibility to feelings and environmental invalidation. Many people are vulnerable to emotion but never develop BPD. Similarly, many people have childhoods that are stressful, disruptive, or even abusive and never develop BPD. In this theory, so to speak, "it takes two to tango." It is also important to note that there is no reason to blame in this theory. Being an emotional person is nothing wrong. There are, in fact, many benefits to being more sensitive.

Sometimes, the most interesting, charismatic persons in the room are very emotional people. They are passionate about life, genuinely feel the pain of others, and are often very empathetic and compassionate. Similarly, people who are less emotional may not know exactly what to do with a very sensitive person, particularly a very emotional child, for no fault of their own. It's like between the invalidating system and the emotional child there is this back and forth. The child becomes really upset, and the parents or carers don't know how to handle it. So the caregivers may tell the child to "stop being so emotional"— not because they want to hurt or upset the child, but because they simply don't know what to do or how to help the child. So, what usually happens when someone tells you shouldn't know what you did? You are definitely going to feel that even more! What's more, you're probably getting angry or defensive or feeling out of balance. You are even more emotional now than you once were. So your caregivers now have even less of an idea of what to do, and they may start feeling themselves out of control, or even frustrated or angry.

Hence, both factors are important according to the biosocial theory, and one can amplify the other. Throughout time, as this occurs over and over again, people who are emotionally vulnerable may start having a lot of trouble controlling their emotions, and they may hate their emotions, consider them overwhelming, and spend a lot of time trying to avoid them. Yes, many people with BPD say they do things like attempted self-harm and suicide to suppress their emotions. Also used for the same reason are alcohol use, binge eating, and other unhealthy behaviors. People with BPD often do these things to feel better in the short term, but, of course, all these behaviors are creating a whole host of long-term problems.

*Validation In DBT*

DBT uses affirmation to help clients feel better understood. Validation means checking that people really think what they're saying and believe what they're saying, they're thinking, as well as demonstrating genuine interest and understanding. DBT therapists are always looking for opportunities to validate the experiences of their clients— to express genuine client interest, understanding, and empathy.

Through DBT, therapists help clients embrace themselves, the world, their feelings and thoughts, and others by teaching skills such as mindfulness, and methods to accept reality for what it is. Now, accepting is not the same as approving, appreciating, liking, or desiring, and certainly does not mean giving up or giving up. To embrace is to let go of the desire to change it, and to allow it to be what it is. For example, you might want to change the way you feel when you're really upset. That is absolutely understandable. The problem is that, no matter how hard we try, sometimes we simply can't change how we feel. Trying to change the feelings in these situations just will make you more upset. There are the same processes at work when we have trouble accepting some aspect of our past. We just can't change our history, as we want. They can't change the fact that we've done things we regret, that we've been through horrible or painful events, or that people close to us have died or left us. The more we try to change those issues, the more they potentially become disturbing. Acceptance, then, is all about dropping the battle against change and allowing things to be as they are — at least for now. Acceptance does not, of course, mean you can't change things that can really be changed. While you can't change your past or get angry, when you get frustrated, you can find ways to take care of yourself and work to solve individual issues in your relationships and overall life (which can help you feel upset less often).

*Change and Problem-Solving in DBT*

DBT is also a problem-solving treatment that involves pushing patients to change in ways that are very (and still very necessary) difficult. DBT is practical and often focuses on solving your life's problems. If you are depressed and have BPD, then something obviously needs to change in your life. Finding a therapist who doesn't help you improve anything would be like asking for directions to a certain location and not getting any directions. When we explain below, approval without improvement is unlikely to be beneficial, nor does change without acceptance work very well.

## What is the Meaning of Dialectical?

Thanks to the focus on balancing acceptance and improvement in treatment, the term dialectical is given center stage in DBT. A dialectic is a tension between the polar opposites— between good and bad, right and wrong, or what you want to do (for example, sitting on a beach and drinking margaritas) and what you need to do (going to work). It can also be the tension between accepting things as they are and changing your life. In a tug-of-war, a dialectic is like rope. In DBT dialectical theory focuses on how these polar opposites come together and form something more complete. For starters, many of us are struggling to balance the demands of our careers with those of our home life. We want to spend more time with our family and our kids, but we also feel pressured to work long hours and spend less time with our families to get the job done well. If we were to go completely to the side of our careers and spend all our time at work, we might excel in our jobs, but there would be shambles in our home life. On the other hand, if we were to spend all our time with our families at home, we would most likely be fired. Therefore, each side (work vs. family) is incomplete on its own, because it doesn't get us what we want to do well on all fronts — namely. Dialectics is the way we achieve this and other goals by balancing and bringing the opposites together. As another example, one of a DBT therapist's main aims is to align client acceptance with the need to help the patient improve his or her life. It's like in a tug-of-war, there are acceptance and transition. If you were constantly pushed by your therapist to improve, you'd probably be fed up, feel invalidated, get upset, and maybe even leave therapy. On the other hand, if all your therapist ever did was tell you how much she understood you, accepted you, and got where you came from, your therapy probably wouldn't go anywhere; if you struggle with BPD (especially if you're suicidal), you know something has to change to make you live a worth living life. Thus, change alone is incomplete due to lack of acceptance, and acceptance alone is incomplete due to a lack of change. The goal of the therapist in DBT is to balance and bring acceptance and change together in a manner that best assists the client.

So, what does Dialectical Behavior Therapy do exactly?

DBT is an integral BPD approach with five key goals, also referred to as DBT's five "functions":

1. Help clients get more motivated to work towards a life worth living, and stop engaging in life-threatening behaviors such as self-harm and attempted suicide

2. Helping clients learn important new skills required to achieve their goals

3. Building a caring atmosphere that facilitates change and development, and having the client organize their life in a way that encourages progress

4. Help therapists stay motivated and empowered to help their clients

5. Help patients translate what they learn in counseling to their real-life outside of treatment

To help customers achieve these goals, DBT requires four primary components:

1. Personal Therapy, 2. Telephone consultation 3. Group skills training 4. Therapist consultation team

**Personal therapy**

Personal therapy normally occurs for about an hour once a week, and mostly focuses on helping you address issues in your life. During DBT, the therapist asks you to complete a form, called a Diary Card every week. On this Diary Card, you keep track of how you feel every day (how depressed you feel, how much happiness you feel), along with any impulses to indulge in self-harm or suicide attempts, any actual self-harm accidents or attempted suicide, and other stuff like whether you are taking your prescription medication properly. In each session, you carry in the Diary Card, and by establishing a hierarchy of recovery objectives, you and your therapist find out what to pay the most attention.

If you have BPD, you may be struggling with being chronically depressed or stressed out, having trouble with your relationships or your job, having panic attacks, engaging in suicidal behavior, etc. Your life may be like a giant messy desk you need to clean up. The desk is cluttered with small pieces of paper, gum wrappers, pens, pencils, half-eaten apples, old calendars, sticky notes, a broken glass, and other things. In fact, it's so messy you get overwhelmed at times, just thinking about where to start. Because you cannot tackle all at once, you need a place to get started. You can start by picking up the broken glass, so you don't hurt yourself in the cleanup process. In DBT, the hierarchy of treatment tells you and your therapist where to begin. And normally you start with the top priority: taking control of life-threatening behavior. Life-threatening behavior is any behavior that poses an impending threat to your life, such as suicide attempts or self-harm. It could also be conduct that affects the lives of others, such as suicidal behavior. The bottom line here is that if you are dead (or, for that matter, if you are in jail for killing someone else), treatment won't help you.

The second most important goal of DBT is non-interfering behavior, which is anything you or the therapist can do that makes it difficult for the treatment to proceed, or to benefit from therapy. Therapy-interfering actions may involve things such as being late in meetings, not attending sessions, not paying attention, screaming at your therapist, or calling your therapist too often. It could mean, for the therapist, not paying attention to you, being absent or ignoring important things, arriving late, missing appointments, forcing you too hard (or too little) to improve, etc. If therapy-interfering behavior occurs, the therapist and the patient discuss it, and find ways to fix it. Ultimately, anything that might interfere with your ability to have a reasonable quality of life is the next most important target. These could involve problems with drugs or alcohol, depression, unemployment, homelessness, and other such issues. In each session, you and your therapist will spend the most time discussing top priority items. And, in each session, the role of your therapist is to help you solve life problems, stay motivated, and keep moving towards the life you want.

**Telephone consultation**

The consultation by telephone is an important part of individual therapy. Where you need help, the individual therapist is available between sessions via telephone, e-mail, or whatever communication method works best for you and the therapist. In DBT, therapists make calls primarily with a view to reducing suicidal crises, helping you learn how to apply a new skill in your daily life, or resolving any conflicts or difficulties between you and therapist. However, if you are in DBT, you and your therapist may also agree to have calls to help you with other issues. You may think of telephone consultation as one way the individual therapist helps you bring therapy into your everyday life.

**Skills Training**

Skills training is a very important part of DBT. The purpose of training skills is to help you learn the skills that you need to improve your life and achieve your goals. Skills training normally occurs in groups of three to twelve clients led by two professionals, and sessions last between 1.5 hours and around 2.5 hours. The first hour or so usually includes reviewing "homework" from the last session, and learning new skills is spent the next hour. The group is pretty much like a class you might take at school. In this way, training classes with DBT techniques are different from some other therapy groups that you may have joined, like a phased program. In process groups, members spend time talking to other members in the group about their emotional reactions, discussing relationships and issues with other members, or discussing their past and how it influences them today, among other topics. DBT groups are much more like schools, compared to method groups. You are organized, and you don't spend time talking to other members of the group about your emotions, your past experiences or your problem actions. The group focuses above all on teaching you important new skills.

Which skills are you learning, then? The DBT abilities include skills in mindfulness, skills in interpersonal effectiveness, skills in emotion regulations, and skills in tolerance of distress. Below is a list of these skills and a brief description of what they entail:

*Mindfulness Skills*

Mindfulness is the state of being fully awake and paying attention to what is happening at the present moment, or "holding one's consciousness alive to the present reality." If you're doing yoga, Pilates, martial arts, or other such activities, you might have had some experience with breathing exercises that involve paying attention to what's going on here and now. The following is a list of the types of DBT skills that fall into the category of mindfulness:

paying attention to the present moment without judging it

Noticing sensations (sights, sounds, smells, tactile sensations) that are happening in the here and now

Describe "just the facts" of what is happening in the present

Throwing yourself fully into what you are doing right now, in the present Focusing on one thing at a time, and doing what works

*Interpersonal Effectiveness Skills*

Interpersonal effectiveness skills are designed to help you manage relationships with other people in an effective manner. As we discussed, one of the issues that follow BPD is the likelihood of having trouble in relationships with others. You may find your relationships are stormy, messy, unsatisfactory, or distressing. You may also notice that sometimes you have trouble asking people what you want or saying no to what others are asking you for. The skills of interpersonal effectiveness are all about effectively navigating relations. They may include: Keeping your goals in mind for your relationships Effectively asking others to do things, or say no to others without being too passive or too aggressive. Validating the feelings of others and being honest, truthful, and fair with others are designed to help you effectively manage your emotions.

*Emotion Regulation Skills*

Emotion regulation skills are designed to help you manage your emotions in an effective manner. As discussed, we agree that the difficulty of controlling feelings is one of the major issues in BPD. You may have noticed that when you feel upset, you just don't know what to do, or that, no matter what you do, you can't make yourself feel any better. Maybe the things that make you feel better (such as drugs, self-harm) cause a lot of other issues too. Skills in regulating emotions are about managing your emotions in ways that work for you and don't cause other issues. These skills might include:

effectively managing your emotions

Observing or accepting your emotions

Changing (increasing or decreasing) your emotional experience

Making yourself less vulnerable to emotions by increasing pleasant events in your life, taking care of yourself and meeting your physical/emotional needs

*Distress Tolerance Skills*

Sometimes, the only thing you can do to get through a hard situation is to tolerate it-at least for the time being. For example, if someone puts a dent in your car, and you can't get to the mechanic for a week or so, you'll probably have to tolerate the fact that your car has a dent. If your partner has just left you, and you are extremely upset, you may need to accept your emotions and the situation until you can find a way to make things better. Skills in distress management are all about tolerating and resolving stressful situations, thoughts, and feelings without making things worse. Distress tolerance skills include:

Working through difficult situations and emotions without making things worse

Surviving challenges through removing yourself from painful experiences or making the current moment happier or more fun

Take reality for what it is

**THERAPIST CONSULTATION TEAM**

Another very important part of DBT is the therapist consultation team. This is a team of professionals who meet, usually once a week, to discuss issues related to using DBT to treat BPD patients. When designing DBT, Dr. Linehan acknowledged that counseling clients who attempt suicide or participate in other self-destructive behaviors could be traumatic to therapists. While therapists care about their clients and wish to do their best to help them, they are also human. It's hard to see people suffering as much as those with BPD do. You know what we are talking about when you have BPD.

You might have noticed that there are times when other people in your life who care about you have difficulty seeing you in so much pain. Thus, it is very important for therapists to have a way to remain inspired so that they can continue to do effective therapy. That is what the counseling team of professionals is all about. The therapist consulting team's philosophy is that all team members handle all clients in the team. So, each team member feels just as responsible for your recovery as does your individual therapist. Therapists help each other stay motivated, act skillfully, and be effective in treating themselves. The team usually includes clinicians who do DBT and see people with BPD or related issues (such as stress control disorders, suicidal behavior, etc.). The team members provide mutual support and encouragement, give each other feedback when their efforts seem to go astray, and monitor whether team members get burned out or use ineffective therapy strategies. Essentially, for therapists, the counseling team is like therapy. Additionally, a client often feels reassured that the therapist has a group of people to help her or him provide the best possible treatment.

# CHAPTER 2:
# MENTALIZATION-BASED TREATMENT

Mentalization-based treatment (MBT) is based on another BPD view. Instead of focusing on emotional issues, MBT focuses on people's sense of who they are, or their "sense of self." Basically, MBT is based on the idea that BPD is the result of a weak self-structure, or unstable sense of self, and poor self-conception. Since MBT and DBT are focused on so many different ideas of what BPD is and how it comes about, you certainly won't be surprised that the ways these therapies seek to help people are also quite different.

*Form of Therapy*

First, MBT is not a cognitive behavioral therapy, but a psychoanalytic therapy. This means MBT is more of a "talk therapy" than a DBT. Most of your time at MBT is spent talking to your therapist and learning about yourself and your relationships with others, rather than learning new skills and doing multiple homework assignments, as you would in DBT. Although you may be walking away from MBT, having picked up some of the same new skills you'd be gaining in DBT, you'd be learning those more indirectly.

*Therapy goals*

The second thing that differentiates MBT from DBT is the purpose of therapy or the aims of treatment. One of the aspects that DBT focuses most on is helping people learn how to control their feelings in a healthy way, rather than doing things that will make their issues worse in the long run (e.g., trying to commit suicide or hurt themselves). The most important goal of MBT, by comparison, is to increase mentalization. Mentalization is the ability to understand that our own actions, and people's behaviors around us, stem from inner mental states such as emotions, feelings, and desires. Essentially, if you've learned how to mentalize, you're able to see that your emotions, feelings, or desires derive from the things you do. These actions aren't coming out of the blue or happening randomly — they are related to how you feel and the thoughts you have. One of the main ideas in MBT is that people with BPD have difficulty understanding how they relate their behaviors to their mental state. People with BPD, for example, might find themselves yelling, or drinking, or hurting themselves and not knowing why they started doing those things, or what was going on inside them that led to those behaviors. If you have BPD, you might feel like "just happen" or "come out of the blue" of your impulsive behaviors. Although it may seem like that, that's generally not what happens.

Alternatively, you may not be conscious of the emotions or thoughts you had before you started to act impulsively, or you may not see the link between your mental states and your actions. The fact that you cannot see this connection doesn't mean it isn't there; it just means you don't know about it. MBT helps you understand this connection between your mental states and behavior. Of course, just as it is important to understand how your actions are linked to your mental states, it is also important to understand how behaviors of other people derive from their mental states. Let's say, for instance, that a young boy's mother screamed at him when she heard he'd been driving while intoxicated. Mentalization would encourage the boy to realize that he was being yelled at by his mother because she was scared and furious and wished he won't do it again. If the boy couldn't mentalize, he might not understand how the shouting from his mother was connected to her feelings and thoughts. Mentalization often includes the ability to comprehend that mental states are related but distinct from behavior. And, for instance, it means being able to understand that the man sitting next to you and crying might be sad, or he might have hurt his feelings, or he might even be angry. And that also means being able to grasp what you are thinking, feeling, and wanting for yourself. Familiar with this last piece? That's possible because, in DBT, it is also very important to understand what you feel and think.

Mentalization of the principle behind MBT is typically acquired gradually during childhood. Kids with loving, caring relationships with their carers develop the ability to mentalize through contact with their parents over the first few years of their lives. The basic idea is for kids to start learning what they think and feel through a mirroring cycle. So, for instance, if a child was with her dad and started crying, he would say, "Oh, are you sad? What went wrong? Why do you feel so sad?"The child would have her emotions reflected and confirmed because of her father's questions and concern in her feelings, and would understand that crying could mean sorrow. This is a great way for children to start learning about their feelings, as it gives them a language for their feelings and also shows them that someone else can understand their feelings and respect them. Children can start applying this mirroring to themselves over time, and ideally start validating and labeling their own feelings.

Now, as mentalization gradually develops over many years, children often experience two states before fully mastering the ability to mentalize. These states represent early attempts by children to understand the relationship between their behaviors and their states of mind.

Psychic equivalence is one such state. People in this state believe that others are just like them, and have the same experiences as they do. It's kind of like seeing the outside world as a direct extension of yourself, including other people. If you're in a state of psychic equivalence, you might think you know all there is to know about the outside world, because it's the same as you are.

Let's assume, for instance, that you're mortally scared of public speaking and have gone to a lecture on some topic. The speaker makes a joke during this lecture, and only a few people in the audience react. If you were in a state of mental equivalence, you may assume the speaker is now mortified and in a state of panic, just because you'd feel those things if you'd be the one speaking up there. The thought that the speaker might not be disturbed by the reaction of the audience would not even cross your mind because you would see the speaker as being your equal (or having the same mental state as you do). One of the psychic equivalence issues is that it can be daunting, because everything can seem so personal and intense. Think about it— Living your own life and having your own experiences can be hard enough. Feeling like you're totally connected to everything around you would probably be quite hard for most people to deal with. The second state people experience before the ability to mentalize has fully developed is called pretend mode. During pretend mode, your state of mind is completely disconnected from the outside world and the rest of your mental states. You may feel really disconnected from yourself, your emotions, and the world around you in this state, and anything may seem unreal. For example, somebody in pretend mode might be able to think about what it would feel like to be sad, or even "try on" the feeling of sadness (by pretending to be sad), when she or he wasn't really feeling that way, and there was no connection with reality or the outside world. It's kind of like someone thinking about feeling sad without ever having any real feeling of sadness in touch. Essentially, at its peak, pretend mode is essentially the same as dissociation. The pretending mode can generally be a very unpleasant and isolating experience.

So how does mentalisation apply to these two states? Well, these states are opposites, as you may have noted, representing two distinct extremes. On the one side, psychic equivalence means feeling as if you're an extension of the universe around you. On the other hand, pretend mode means feeling isolated or cut off from yourself and from the world around you.

Mentalization balances these two states in some ways so that you can understand yourself and others better. With mentalization, the inner and outer worlds of individuals are seen as connected but separate from one another. In other words, people understand that they are not the same thing as their internal states and the outside world, but they also know that they are not completely unrelated. And, if you can mentalize, you'd realize that your actions (for example, shouting or waving at someone) are linked to your feelings and thoughts, that these actions can trigger reactions in other people (such as rage or happiness), and that these reactions can then cause these other people to respond in some way (for example, yelling back at you or smiling at you).

## The Development of BPD as Seen Through the Lens of MBT

To date, we have identified how children develop mentalization under good conditions by engaging with loving parents and caring caregivers. The concern is that not all children are brought up in ideal conditions, and not all children have the opportunity to interact with loving parents, so this skill is not established by all children. People learn to understand and explain their internal states by having someone around them who constantly expresses what they think and feel back to them. Therefore, if you don't have someone around you who does that — and is doing it fairly accurately— it can be very hard to learn about your own thoughts and feelings. So, let's pretend you're a kid, and you've come home from school feeling really angry because your lunch was thrown out by another child in the schoolyard. In this case, if your mom were to provide objective mirroring, she would tell you that you look angry and ask you what happened to make you feel that way. This would help you to learn about your angry feelings. On the other hand, if your mom laughed at you or said you looked scared, you'd probably get confused and feel misunderstood. And, that would certainly make it more difficult to know what rage really is. In reality, inaccurate mirroring is sort of like an invalidating atmosphere. In fact, children learn more about who they are and how they feel when they are around people who accurately reflect their feelings and thoughts back to them. So, as you can see, although DBT and MBT approach these issues in different ways, both of these treatments are based on the idea that being around caregivers who don't understand how you feel, or who can't validate your feelings and help you understand them, can lead to problems. So, what if your loved ones or caregivers do not consistently and accurately mirror your internal states when you grow up? Well, people develop their sense of who they are through these mirroring interactions with their parents or caregivers, according to MBT. Therefore, if your parents or caregivers say you feel or think something you are not, you may be confused about who you really are. In fact, you might start developing a sense of who you are that actually doesn't match who you really are.

Let's say you're an outgoing person, for instance, but you're told over and over that you're shy and scared around others. If you're told this often enough, you might start believing you're actually a shy person, even if you're not. Since children develop a sense of who they are partially based on what their parents are reflecting back to them, children whose caregivers do not represent the right things may end up feeling confused about who they are. Consequently, they can find it difficult to establish a secure identity or sense of self. What's more, when you're trying to develop a sense of self-based on inaccurate information, you're not only going to be confused about who you are, but you'll probably also feel very detached or alienated from yourself. The problem with inaccurate mirroring is that the information that is being reflected back to you is actually less about you and more about the reflective person. So, if you try to base your sense of who you are on this inaccurate information, it's just not going to feel right the sense of self you end up with. It's like trying to squeeze a square peg into a spherical hole— it's just not going to work! The word alien self was used to characterize the part of the self that is formed on the basis of incorrect mirroring because it is so different from who the individual really is. Moreover, since the alien self often reflects the negative image of or negative feelings towards the person by the caregiver (such as frustration), this alien self will be not only different but also disturbing. Because it can be so unsettling, most people will want to do all they can to get rid of their alien selves and push it away.

## The Dilemma of the "Alien Self"

Unfortunately, no matter if you see the alien self as part of you and try to keep it inside, or try to get rid of the alien self and push it away, there's no good solution. If your alien nature persists within you, it will disjoint your sense of self. What's more, because the alien self is really about the feelings and beliefs of someone else about you (rather than who you are), it often seems like someone else's governs it, which can be a pretty disturbing experience! On the other hand, if you try to push your alien self away from you and into the outside world (through a psychological process called projection), you're still not in the safe. Since the alien self holds the negative feelings about you that your caregiver has, bringing it into the outside world means that the outside world will now have negative feelings about you. In turn, people who try to get rid of this part of themselves by forcing it out of them set up to view the outside world as angry, aggressive and threatening— another unsettling experience.

## Mentalization and BPD

So how does BPD apply to all of this? Well, experts believe that BPD is caused by a failure to develop mentalization, leading to problems with the sense of self (specifically, a weak self-structure) of the individual. It's those self-problems that contribute to many of the BPD symptoms. According to MBT, people with BPD can't mentalize when they're in a state of emotional anticipation or are really angry. They must have recourse to other ways of making sense of themselves and others during these times. Especially since people with BPD are unable to mentalize during periods of intense anxiety, they rely on the use of emotional equivalence and pretend mode to retain a sense of self during stressful times. Nonetheless, many of the impulsive actions that people with BPD frequently struggle with are considered to be a futile attempt to protect themselves and somehow to cope with the alien selves. People with BPD, for example, may get overwhelmed by the negative and harsh alien self within them. Because it's so terrible to have an alien self, a person with BPD will injure him or herself in an attempt to punish or kill this alien self (and build a stronger or more coherent self-sense). Conversely, someone with BPD may attempt to get rid of the alien self by forcing it out into the outside world (where it is often perceived as part of someone else). In this situation, the person with BPD may lash out at that other individual in an effort to once and for all kill the alien self. That is one of the main reasons why people with BPD have such stormy relationships, according to MBT.

What can I expect from MBT, then?

MBT is a comprehensive therapy designed initially as a limited hospital program. The number of hours a week spent in partial hospital treatment comes somewhere between hospital services and regular outpatient therapy. The MBT part-hospital program includes six hours of structured care per week, including one hour of individual therapy, three-hour group therapy sessions, one hour of interactive therapy, and a community meeting. Clients receive one individual therapy session and one group therapy session per week in this new outpatient form of MBT, for a total of two and a half hours of treatment a week.

*Individual therapy*

If you are taking part in individual MBT therapy, you may expect your therapist to try hard to get you to think about why you are doing the things you are doing, and how others might react to those actions. The therapist could ask you, for example, to think about how she or he would feel about something you did, and then to focus on how these thoughts and feelings might lead to different actions. Your therapist may also spend time thinking about and explaining how your actions derive from your emotions, feelings, and desires. All in all, an MBT therapist should work with you to help you understand the actions of all come from or are linked to some internal experience, such as emotions, feelings, or desires. The therapist should also also spend a great deal of time trying to understand how the actions relate to your thoughts and feelings, and how your thoughts and feelings contribute to her or his counseling actions. The concept is that the efforts of your therapist to explain how your behaviors are linked to other people's actions (and to your feelings and thoughts about their actions) will also help you understand those relationships. To put it another way, you might learn to mentalize. Let's assume, for instance, that your therapist is trying to understand how your session's crying is linked to something she or he just said, and to your feelings of sadness and anxiety about this comment. Your therapist's efforts to understand these links can help you begin to learn how your actions (in this case, crying) are connected to the things that happen around you and your responses to these things, according to the concepts of MBT. It is also worth mentioning that MBT therapists are encouraged to apply the treatment techniques to themselves, as in DBT. MBT therapists are basically trained to understand how their own responses and attitudes in the session are related to their mental state and the activities of the client. MBT therapists are supposed to do exactly what they are asking their clients to do in this manner, so the purpose of mentalization is present for all. This really adds to the sense that you and your therapist are working and working together in a collaborative relationship, which is a very important thing to have in therapy. Finally, keep in mind that both you and your therapist will spend a lot of time wondering and curious about how actions and mental states relate to each other, rather than assuming either one of you has all the answers or fully understands what the other person experiences. This is called taking a "not knowing" position and is considered important to help clients develop mentalization.

*What is Group Therapy About?*

We spoke about the kinds of things that you could find in individual MBT therapy. Because MBT focuses on mentalization, you'll also find many of these issues in group therapy. You can think of MBT group therapy as the same as MBT individual therapy in some ways–just with more people in the room! As discussed, in MBT group therapy, all group members (and the group leader) should take a "not knowing" stance and will try their best to understand how the actions of group members are linked to the activities of other group members, as well as their own emotions, thoughts, and desires. In particular, it would allow all members of an MBT community to recognize the mental states of the other group members, as well as their own mental states. For instance, clients would be asked to consider why they think another member of the group feels the way they do, or why they are acting in a particular way. In reality, group therapy provides a great opportunity to practice this ability because of the emphasis on mentalization (which really involves thinking about other people in relation to ourselves).

# CHAPTER 3:
# COPING WITH YOUR EMOTIONS

Look up and picture a colorful kite on a windy day soaring out into the sky. Blue sky, a few wisps of clouds, it's all peaceful and quiet, but the kite is unexpectedly caught by a wind roaring. The kite is spinning off balance and falling to the ground. Those with borderline personality disorder (BPD) have an emotional life that looks much like kites. Occasionally they fly high, but they spin out of control and fall quickly like a kite.

*Putting a Name Tag on Emotions*

A lot of people have difficulty identifying and respecting their emotions. Yet it's perfectly normal not to note your emotional state at any moment. Most of the time, you don't think consciously about how you feel unless you're extremely sad, frustrated, scared, or satisfied. For instance, has someone ever asked you, "Why are you in a foul mood today?" And you answer,' I'm not in a bad mood,' without thought, really? Instead, a few minutes later, you remember that you actually felt irritable and somewhat crabby (not that you would admit it). And your response was not a lie, or an attempt to hide your feelings. You dismissed the thought unconsciously because you were not consciously aware of your bad mood.

*Understanding the connection between your thoughts and feelings*

So what's the big deal if you don't think about what you feel? Feelings are deep communication tools— they keep people connected to each other, and that connection brings forth life and love. Feelings are positive and advise caution. They tell us, essentially, how to behave. For instance,

When people grieve, they tend to retreat.

When people are afraid, they defend or run.

When people are angry, they attack.

When people are curious, they explore.

When people are joyful, they celebrate.

However, while feelings influence how you conduct yourself, they can also become overwhelming and unhelpful when your thoughts do not match them. Both thoughts and feelings should play a role in your actions because thoughts are helping to change feelings. When your sensations determine your actions without any input from your thoughts, your actions are unmodified by wisdom and can lead you into trouble.

*Practicing emotional regulation*

Over time the ability to control emotions and alter habits improves. A baby behaves according to his emotions, for example, not his ideas. When a kid gets upset, he cries; he laughs when he's happy; he throws a tantrum when he's mad. When he matures, his emotional gestures become more nuanced— he does not cry each time he gets upset— and instead, he may complain or ask his parents for help. He realizes he's got other options to show off his feelings. If he develops normally, he begins to think about how he feels and how to express himself by the time he is in elementary school. So, he might get angry at a playground playmate but desist from hitting him. Or, he may feel hurt by bullying someone, but he doesn't burst into tears.

Furthermore, even as time goes by, people with BPD do not necessarily master the art of emotional regulation. Ultimately, emotions take over and control people's behavior with BPD because they have no idea how to change feelings with thoughts. Thoughts and feelings are not associated for them, and their ability to balance feelings and regulate outbursts is disturbed by this disconnection. Understandably, most people with BPD feel fraught with uncertainty in their emotional lives. Feelings can be positive as happiness or negative as sorrow or a combination of both, but from a moral standpoint, they are not inherently good or bad. If you have difficulty identifying and explaining what you feel and how you feel, keep a few weeks of daily logging. Take three to five times daily for a couple of moments to write down how you feel at that particular time. Notice the sensations in your body that go with your feelings. Identify your emotions, your physical feelings, the situation when making your note, and any thoughts you might have. Don't worry about your grammar and the punctuation. Write fast without too much thinking. If you are on medication, speak with your therapist about your performance.

Relaxing and Practicing Frequent, intensely negative emotions take a toll on your body because your body prepares for danger every time you feel a strong negative emotion and gets ready to run or fight it. Those with BPD show more negative emotions and less positive emotions than the majority of others do. Such highly negative feelings are debilitating, and the chances for the following health problems increase:

High blood pressure

Chronic headaches

Muscle aches

Type 2 diabetes

Back pain

Irritable bowel syndrome

Acid reflux

Depressed immune system

Heart disease

Stroke

The basic reason behind managing emotions is based on a biological reality by learning how to relax: you can not be both calm and frenzied at the same time. Your body slows down when you're in a state of relaxation, your heart rate decreases, your muscles relax, and you have time to reflect. Relaxation also helps people gain control over their emotions. In the next sections we describe several relaxation ideas and methods.

*Making muscles relax*

Basically, this process involves stretching a group of muscles and then letting out the tension. You should pay attention to the group of muscles that you are tensing and then note how they react when releasing the stress. This simple technique can help almost anyone. Of course, if you have problems with your back, arthritis, muscle pain, or have been injured, check with your health care provider before trying this technique Getting ready to relax if you are considering this technique of muscle relaxation, keep in mind the following tips:

Find a secluded spot and switch off your cell phone.

Do not use substances that influence your mind.

Do not have a full stomach.

Wear clothing that is loose-fitting.

If your feet start to get cold, wear socks.

Try to keep your expression calm knowingly.

Stop if you experience pain while your muscles are tensed.

Focus on the comfortable feeling as you loosen your muscles.

If during this exercise you feel very nervous, stop.

When you fall asleep, don't worry; just resume when you wake up.

Don't claim to be perfect; this approach should be soothing after all.

Expect some time to master the method.

*Full progressive relaxation of muscles*

You can begin with full progressive relaxation of the muscles. Even though you don't really have to follow the directions in this section, they will help you get started. You will be able to utilize progressive muscle relaxation without a manual after you practice a few times. If you choose to use this technique to help you gain control over your strong emotions, you should practice it for at least one week or longer every day. You should work on a shorter version after you have practiced enough times, and gradually you will be able to deliberately relax your muscles without any structured procedures at all.

Follow these steps to begin full progressive muscle relaxation:

1. Get relaxed and just take some breaths. Inhale through your nose, deeply. Hold your breath for a couple of seconds; then exhale slowly. Each time it is suggested that you tense your muscles, hold the tension for about 10 seconds. When suggested, you let go of the tension and relax, focus 10 or 15 seconds on relaxation. But don't be uptight with the exact time, and don't use a stopwatch!

2. Begin with your feet. Curl your toes; strain your feet with all your muscles. Relax now. Concentrate on your feet feeling relaxed.

3. Moving up, relax your calves by bringing your heels down and pointing your toes towards your

nose. When you feel some discomfort, watch out for muscle cramps, and stop. Release; feel the tension flowing out of your calves.

4. Squeeze thighs down. Keep on, and let go.

5. Squeeze your buttocks. Keep on concentrated. Relax, and feel the relief.

6. Pull the abdomen in. Imagine rubbing the spine with your belly button. Tighten up; release then. Feel bad energy flowing away.

7. Create fists and squeeze. Let go. Note the feeling.

8. Tighten the muscles in your arm. Push the upper arms near to the body. Hold out your forearms as if you were holding something up in front of you. Use all your strength; let your arms fall now, and release tension.

9. You'll need to use two different movements to calm your shoulders. Lift your shoulders up first and try to touch your mouth. Keep on, and let go. Then pull back your shoulder blades and

stick the chest out. Only think about hitting your shoulders behind you. Then just relax.

10. Do not push too hard with your neck, and do not try this if you have whiplash or any type of neck injury. Drive the neck down into the arms. Hold back and relax. Move them to one side now. Tilt your head to one shoulder; hold and release. Now, on the other hand, follow the same motion— ear to neck. Eventually, pull your head back gently towards your back, then release.

11. Now for your face. Scrunch— squeeze your forehead, jaw, tongue, and lips. Relax and unwind.

12. Just imagine going through an inventory of your muscles with your eyes closed. Repeat the muscle tension-and-release process, if you still feel the tension in any place. Breathe for a few minutes, and feel relaxed.

Most people will feel discomfort in the arms, back, or neck. Feel free to change or increase the number of times you are tensioning and releasing those areas. As an instant stress reducer, you might also want to tense and relax an area in your body several times a day.

Shortened muscle relaxation Try putting muscle groups together after you have practiced the muscle relaxation as depicted in the previous section. See if the following method will help you achieve relaxation.

1. Get cozy, and take some deep breaths.

2. Squeeze all muscles down from your waist. Squeeze the knees, curl the feet and pinch the thighs. Keep the stress for ten seconds or so; then relax.

3. Pull in your stomach, and try to push your back (or chair) into the floor. Hold, and then release, feeling your tension flowing away.

4. Press your arms into your body, squeeze your hands, and push up your ears to your shoulders. Imagine warm water waves softly rolling over you, as you relax.

5. Squeeze your face's muscles-grin, grimace, and squint. Keep tight muscles, and then relax.

6. Stay conscious of your body. There are areas of tension in there? If so, muscles in those areas are tensed and released. Breathe in and have fun. Remember how you feel about your body.

## CHAPTER 4:
## DEALING WITH SUICIDAL THOUGHTS

When you think about suicide regularly, breaking the habit may be very difficult for you. It's as if your brain gets used to thinking about suicide every time there's a big enough problem going through the door. You might find it soothing to think about suicide, just like you've got an escape valve that you can use if things get too hard or you lose hope. In fact, thinking about suicide for some people can actually become like a reflection — something bad happens, and Voila! The mind thinks of suicide straight away. Changing a reflex-like that can, of course, be very difficult. Occasionally, the thoughts only come too quickly for you to be able to stop them. So, don't expect you'll never think about suicide again if you use these skills. That may not happen. But what could happen is you'll know how not to rely on your emotions, and you'll feel like you have more flexibility to choose what you're doing.

Stay away from "Harmful Means"

One of the very first things you should do when you think about suicide is get away from harmful means — anything you could use to kill yourself. People who think a lot about suicide generally have a fairly clear picture of what they would do to kill themselves. When you know what you'd be doing, then be sure to immediately remove yourself from those lethal means. The premise here is that if you don't have access to the tools or techniques you would use to do the job, you will be far less likely to attempt suicide. Below are some ways of keeping yourself out of the way of harm: If you want to overdose your medicines, then get out of your home and away from your medicines, flush them down the toilet (you can always get later), give them to someone else for safekeeping until the crisis has passed, or lock them up somewhere it would be difficult for you to get them on the spur of the moment. If you want a knife or other sharp object to hurt yourself, get these things out of your house, or get away from them. Don't allow yourself to buy things you'd be using to harm yourself. Don't let yourself drive "accidentally" past the store where you could buy razor blades or medicines. Don't "accidentally" end up in the home of your drug dealer, where you can buy drugs for an overdose.

*Think About What You Really Want*

When you have thoughts of suicide, it is best if you think about what you really want first. Do you want to be dead, or do you want to feel better, or do you want to get rid of a problem that bothers you? In one of her videos on DBT, Dr. Marsha Linehan said, "If you're talking of suicide, that means there's a problem." Many people with BPD say they're trying to commit suicide to relieve their thoughts, or that other people's feelings are better off. You may think the same thing— that if you kill yourself, you're going to feel more at ease, you're no longer going to have to deal with your issues, or you're going to make it, so other people don't have to deal with you or worry about you anymore. But what if you're able to solve those issues and not end up dead in the process? Still, wanting to be dead? What if there was some way more often to feel more happy or satisfied, feel more in control of your life, and solve your problems?

Would you like to kill yourself anyway? If you notice that you are considering suicide, figure out what you really want. Start with the following steps:

1. Say, "Yeah, a suicidal thought. This appears to mean there's an issue."

2. Find out what the issue is. There could be anything to the issue. It could be that something very traumatic has just happened to you (for example, a girlfriend broke up with you), and you feel awful and don't know what to do about it. And, it could be that you've long felt discouraged and can't see any way out of it. The important thing here is to get yourself to think about the question that might drive those suicidal thoughts on.

3. Find what you wish for. As we have said, you might want your problem to go away a lot of time, or you might want to feel more contented or more peaceful. So instead, say to yourself, "I don't want to be gone, I just want to." Fill in the blank with your primary wishes, like "feel more calm," "feel better," "ignore my feelings," "stop thinking about my issues," or "find a way to make things better."

4. The next step is to figure out what you can do without killing yourself to get what you want. If you can't come up with something on your own, then use some of the skills in this book, look around for other coping skills that could help, call a friend or someone who can give you good advice, or talk to your therapist, if you have one.

5. Recall that killing yourself is an enduring solution to a temporary problem. Life takes us all by surprise. What if it's just around the next corner to solve your problem, and you never get there because you killed yourself?

When therapists see patients with suicidal thoughts, often, the first thing they ask them is, "Would you like to be dead, or would you like to escape the pain that you are in right now?" Everyone asked this question has said," I want to be out of pain. "No one has said," I want to be dead. "The clients tell their therapist they are not thinking of suicide unless their intention is to die. Rather, they simply can not come up with another way of feeling better or of solving their problems. Sometimes people see suicide as the solution in this way, rather than the problem. Yet note, there are plenty of other options, plenty of other ways out of the pain. You've just got to find them. And you may need some support for that— from a therapist, a friend, a family member, a case manager, or perhaps such a self-help book as this one.

*Change the situation*

You'd be amazed at what a difference you can make in and out of the environment, you're in. If you're thinking about suicide at home, leave and go somewhere, preferably with others around (a restaurant, coffee shop, store, library, university, and so on). But the important thing here is: don't spend time thinking about going anywhere— just do it. As soon as you think you have to leave your place (or wherever you are), just choose a safe place and get out now while you can — before convincing yourself not to do so! When you get to where you're headed, pay attention to what's happening around you, rather than being lost in your head all the time. So look out for all the sights, sounds, smells, and tastes about everything around you. That will allow you to experience the world from another perspective.

*Take Action and Question Hopeless Thinking*

Time and again, research studies have shown that suicidal thoughts and actions are predicted by hopeless thoughts about the future. Suicidal people tend to think about their lives with more hopeless thoughts than people who don't think about suicide. Most importantly, suicidal people are less likely than nonsuicidal people to think that something good will happen in the future. They are also less able to come up with reasons why there will be no negative events in the future. It can be incredibly difficult to think clearly when you are mired in strong, negative emotions and hopeless thinking could dominate your mind. But, at those moments, thinking positive thoughts still won't be easy for you. You may find that you continue to "poison" any optimistic thoughts that you come up with, such as saying, "I don't believe it. Nothing will ever improve. "However, the best way to deal with helpless thoughts when you are in the midst of an emotional crisis is to take action right now and stop feeling hopeless.

The best acts to take when you think of hopeless thoughts are those which tell you that things can actually improve. One skill you can use to hopeless thinking involves "acting the opposite." In Dialectical Behavior Therapy (DBT) with Dr. Marsha Linehan, one of the important skills used to help people manage their emotions is called "opposite action," which involves acting in a way that is the opposite of what you feel like doing. So, if you're upset with someone and feel like shouting at them, the opposite behavior would be to be kind to the person. If you're afraid and feel like fleeing the situation, it would be the opposite move to live in the situation. When you think things are bleak than act contrary to those hopeless thoughts. When you were very hopeful that things could get better, think about what you would do. Instead, take immediate action to make things better. You may not be able to solve your life issues right now, but you may be able to do something to make you feel better, take a small step to solve your problem or try to understand what's going on in your lifetime.

So, if you've got hopeless feelings, go through any of the skills, choose one, and act. Call a relative, talk to your therapist— do whatever you can to get an idea of the first step you can take. Even taking the slightest step towards improving things will boost your attitude and give you hope things can change. But here's an important point to remember: this only works if you pay real attention to what's going on. Do not take a small step but spend the whole time stuck in your head worrying about how bad or horrible things are, or how much you want to kill yourself. Keep your eyes and mind open to what's going on around you right now, and look out for the small but important steps you are taking.

*Let the Thoughts Come and Go*

Another ability that can be of great help is clearly to let the suicidal thoughts come and go. The fact that you're having suicidal thoughts doesn't mean you need to act on those feelings. They are just feelings— the mind's operation. We all have feelings we never would be acting on. You may feel angry with your boss and talk about yelling or throwing things at her or him, but (we hope!) you don't act on these thoughts. Thoughts are merely feelings. Often, they are very convincing. They sound and feel true, and it might seem like the thing to do is kill yourself. But you have the right just to let your thoughts come and go and not act on them. Below is one exercise you can use to bring this technique into practice: Imagine you're lying in a large green field and gazing up to the sky. It is a warm and sunny, peaceful day, with a slight breeze. You see some big, bubbling white clouds floating along in the sky. Imagine your thoughts being written on each cloud, and watching the clouds float by. Let them just go. Don't pursue any cloud (or thought). Let them just go.

# CHAPTER 5:
# HELPING YOURSELF AND OTHERS

If you have BPD, your relationships with friends were probably turbulent, dysfunctional, and unsatisfactory. Intimate relationships were probably downright disastrous. Good relationships, in general, have enormous benefits for people. Research shows that people with social networks that support them have better physical and mental health, as well as longer lives. Indeed, having people to speak with also seems to protect against loss of early memory. Building better partnerships should be an integral part of your plan to surmount BPD with so many natural benefits.

The most critical interpersonal skill of all is the ability to understand that while other people, like you, have thoughts, opinions, and emotions, these thoughts, opinions, and emotions are not always compatible with your own.

You run a high risk of insulting, disrespecting, harming, or upsetting them when you fail to grasp where others are coming from. You can also bore people by focusing on your own problems and failing to notice the signs that tell you it's time to communicate with whomever you speak.

This interpersonal ability includes both recognizing that other people have individual feelings and thoughts, and appreciating that other people have different motives and goals that they don't necessarily state clearly and specifically. Being able to understand other people's perspectives and mindsets allows you to do the following:

Empathize with others

Make sense of what others do

Adapt your behavior in response to how others react

Predict how others will likely respond to you

Understand nuances in conversations such as humor, irony, and teasing

Adjust what you say according to feelings

Sympathy happens when you express a sense of care or concern for a person or even a group of individuals. For starters, you could be sympathetic to the homeless's plight. Empathy, by comparison, involves being able to picture oneself in the position of another person. You may be empathetic because at some point in your life, you experienced a similar occurrence, or because you can genuinely put yourself in the shoes of someone else. Empathy tends to be an abstract thinking ability that differs among people— some people simply tend to be more empathic than others naturally.

**Projection:** That someone feels what you feel people with BPD are forming coping strategies that can turn out to be quite self-defeating in the long run. One of those forms of coping involves taking their own stressful, negative feelings or characteristics and projecting them onto another. In so doing, they hope to avoid their bad feelings by giving them to someone else.

**Reducing projecting events**

If you have a propensity to transfer your own feelings onto others, you can use the practice to will it. To maximum effectiveness, though, you can combine your own efforts with therapy work. The decreasing projection process begins with increasing the self-awareness, or truthful emotional evaluation and assessment. Look back at the rough experiences with others of your experience. Ask yourself if you accused others of having feelings which reflected how you felt about yourself? If so, you want to avoid this pattern from destroying or interfering with your current and future relationships. You also want to change your emotions, especially anger and rage. Try to note the responses of your body (such as muscle tension in your arms, neck, or jaw, rapid heart rate, flushing, and sweating) that occur before you say anything important or strike someone. When you get struck by those physical emotions, postpone doing anything at all costs! Delaying your initial reaction could help you take a few slow, deep breaths, rather than lashing out.

Ask yourself a few questions after you postpone your reaction:

Could I be angry with myself?

Has anything lately made me feel ashamed?

Am I afraid of something?

Am I worried somebody's going to leave me?

If you answer yes to any of these questions, then your indignation may be more about your own issues than the other person. Try to make one of the following changes, or less provocative statements, rather than lashing out: I feel emotional right now; I need to get back to you on this.

I need to take a break before we go further with this.

Before I comment on this, I have some things to think about.

I hear you, and I promise that when I feel better, I'll discuss it with you.

It's a longstanding tendency to get upset with others because of your own feelings of shame and anger for yourself. It takes a lot of time and practice to change such enduring patterns— not to mention effort. Give yourself some time, and don't expect immediate outcomes.

*PRACTICING PERSPECTIVE TAKING*

While not thinking that other people feel as you feel about yourself is a valuable skill to master, taking perspective often allows you to learn how to understand the state of minds of other people— that is, their thoughts and feelings. In the following sections, we look at a couple of approaches to work on this capacity.

*TAKING TURNS*

The strength of anxiety, as emotions run high, appears to absorb all of your focus and attention. And, sadly, in people with BPD, the emotions still run-heavy. Think of the brain as having only so much room — thinking skills are overwhelmed when packed with emotion. At such moments, it's hard to fight the urge to chat on and on to whoever will listen to you about anything you feel. But if you put yourself in that tentation, you probably miss seeing that the person you're talking to is anxious, frustrated, and/or burnt out.

One way to combat this tendency is to focus on pushing yourself to "take turns" in most of your interactions, if not all. Just as parents teach their children to share and take turns, as you converse with other people, you need to train yourself to turn around. You are likely to learn a lot about what the person you're talking to thinks and feels about in the process. A good rule of thumb is to try to take up half the conversation time and let the other half take up the person you are talking with. Asking a lot of questions can help you achieve that goal.

*ASKING QUESTIONS*

They are far more likely to feel interested in you when you show interest in other people. Not only do questions keep discussions going, but they also help you show the person you're talking to that you're interested in him and the subject you're dealing with. The answers to your questions can then be used to infer what the other person might think.

Try listening to the answers attentively when you ask questions. Consider following up on the answer with another question concerning what you have learned. Often, doing so keeps the conversation going, and keeps both parties engaged.

Try not to interpret your actions as hostile when people answer your questions, and do your best to hold back your defensive responses. Maybe you wonder what kind of questions you're going to ask people. While nearly every query can be helpful, you may want to expand on a few examples. The following list is applicable to many different situations, although far from exhaustive:

Can you tell me more about that?

How have you done this?

Is this something about which you feel strongly?

How do you think about this?

Tell me something about yourself. (Okay, this one isn't exactly a question, but it serves the same goal.) Have you ever come across something like that in your lifetime?

How are you doing this sort of thing?

Work hard to ask your questions in an inquisitive, gentle tone. Evite some sarcasm hint or accusatory slant. Failure to do so may defeat the purpose of helping you develop relationships and maintain them.

*Considering different significances and motives*

People with BPD appear to misinterpret the definitions and purpose of the expressions of other people. All too often, they infer aggressive, threatening motives from others' words. The misinterpretation is known as the presumption of malice. A counterattack is almost inevitable, if you make a false statement. Work with your therapist to review some of your previous conversations, which turned out to be bad. The therapist can help you create less cynical and judgmental views, which are more likely to be correct, as a matter of fact.

When you find yourself making false assumptions, there are many unpleasant experiences that you are likely to have. Not only do these assumptions make you unhappy, but they also add to your life's tension. Besides, negative perceptions are taking a toll on the efficiency of all your relationships.

Malicious assumptions do sometimes prove to be true. In other words, people are expressing very animosity at times. Yet by trusting in the non-judgmental premises, you have nothing to lose. More often than not, your non-judgmental intuition is right, so you avoid turning an innocuous discussion into an argumentative fiasco by holding back your hostile accusation–thereby preventing a counterattack. Not to mention the partnerships can be maintained or strengthened too.

Many people with BPD often do not fully appreciate or even consider how their behavior affects the people who care about them. Because their own overwhelming emotions consume their attention, they are not carefully attending to the reactions of other people. These breakdowns in communication are part of the cycle of expression–disconnection–rejection, which begins when people with BPD overly focus on expressing their own emotions and concerns. Many people feel a lack of communication with them as their interactions wear on, and as a result, they may eventually condemn the people with BPD.

In reality, if you have BPD, you run a high risk of being rejected by others.

The explanation for this rejection, however, is not because you're a horrible person. It is because you might not understand how other people are affected by your actions or words. One way to begin recognizing the effect on others is to begin looking at the faces of the people. A task where different words are heard see if, when people are tired, distracted, annoyed, excited, sad, optimistic, happy, and really angry, you can work out the difference in facial expressions or not. Pay attention also to the sounds and movements of other people's voices. Start this practice with people who talk to others, then apply your skills to people who talk to you. Although recognizing your impact on other people is an important step towards achieving your overall goal of knowing others better, you also need to work to reduce defensiveness.

*Decreasing Defensiveness*

Defensiveness refers to the practice of using retaliatory comments to fend off perceived threats, assaults, and criticism. This is not physical attacks we are talking about here. Rather, about the moments when you view others as dismissive of you. Individuals with BPD frequently respond by counterattacking to these perceived attacks, which may include blaming others or turning up the heat on the conversation by lacing the vocabulary with sarcasm or aggression. Note that anyone who experiences a fit of intense anger is far less able to accurately think or understand interactions than someone who feels calm and relaxed. The reactions of people who are extremely angry are 99.2 percent of the time inappropriate. Your reasoning skills are just not at full capacity when you're angry and upset. The three following techniques will help you fight defensiveness.

*Quit Focusing on Just Yourself*

Defensive people keep focusing on themselves. They do not necessarily believe that they are better or more important than others, but in a sense, they do believe the world revolves around them. They are constantly in the spotlight, in other words— but that spotlight can shine far too brightly. Consider all the good and bad things that happen to affect your feelings and moods when everything in life has personal significance. Taking things too personally is a common communication problem, especially for people with personality disorders, including BPD. Here are a few examples of this problem in action:

A patron at a restaurant becomes furious when she has to wait for service because a couple of the wait staff called in sick, and there aren't enough waiters available for the crowd. She is so rude to her waiter that she embarrasses others at her table. The waiter apologizes and explains they are staffed short, but the patron refuses to accept the apology. Then she thinks the restaurant is singling her out for bad treatment in some way.

A driver gets frustrated when a train moving delays his transport to work. His blood pressure is rising as he watches the train pass by before him. He is wondering why trains always seem to interrupt his commute when it is late.

An ER physician calls a neurologist to schedule a consultation with him and becomes sarcastic and angry when the neurologist asks the patient a few questions before scheduling the meeting. The ER doctor feels personally offended by the reluctance of the neurologist to hop into his car and arrive in the ER without challenging the decision of the doctor. After his computer keyboard stops working, a man gets mad. His frustration interferes with his desire to get back to work after he has got a substitute. He says he experiences computer problems far more often than they should.

The key issue in all three cases is that each person believes the event has somehow a negative, personal significance. Even random events such as computer breakdowns and train intersections become personal. If, in these examples, you tend to personalize things as do the people, it is time to work on this issue. The following steps may help:

1. Slow down, and take two or three deep and slow breaths.

2. Ask yourself if the unpleasant incident really is focused on you, or if it may be just circumstances or bad luck.

3. Tell yourself if being upset and angry would offer you any benefits.

4. Ask if your rage, for that matter, could hurt someone around you or yourself.

5. Try reminding yourself, "Stuff always happens— it's not all about me." Having a friend on your side Some of our patients, over the years, find our second strategy surprisingly effective in overcoming defensiveness. This technique asks you to imagine an objective observer in a clutch sitting on your shoulder to give you sage advice and guidance. The role of your observer is to note when you feel frustrated, upset, or in danger. Your therapist

should give you some helpful advice at those times, such as:

Slow down. When you speak right now, you will make things much worse.

So what would you lose if he's not attacking you?

Let's try something different this time from the normal blow up, all right?

Remember, I'm here to help? Alternatively, say something positive.

How many times has the problem helped to explode?

What's he going to think and feel if you're doing that? How would you react if you had someone telling you that?

How about you actually trying to encourage him, instead of tearing him apart as you wish? Having listened to the advice of your target analyst, work hard to follow it! If you practice it, this technique can really help you. The first few times you try it, it is not likely to work well, but over time you will hear these calming words coming more and more often from the observer. Some people pinpoint on an index card the preceding phrases and read them every day to remind their objective observer to use them when things start to deteriorate.

*Musing over defusing*

It is called defusing, which is a great alternative to becoming defensive. If you view someone as dismissive of you, defusing will keep things calm rather than encourage escalation. Defusing means doing the opposite of what you feel like doing: you try to find a sliver of reality in what the other person has just told you, rather than counterattacking. You keep the dialog going and slowly let the steam out of the conversational pressure cooker, which may have been ready to explode when you show the actual agreement of a small part (sometimes even all) of what someone has said.

*Getting Along Better*

People with BPD also lack the social skills to maintain and cultivate healthy interpersonal relationships. Loss and tension are often a part of their romantic lives. This section describes some basic ways to improve interactions within society. If you have BPD, you can exercise these skills with friends or acquaintances. Try to increase your interpersonal skills with people you don't have intimate relationships with before trying to work on closer relationships. Expect those approaches at first to feel very awkward and uncomfortable. With a little practice, though, you'll probably find that they're becoming second nature.

*Listening*

Listening to others not only transmits interest but also helps to develop your skills in taking perspective. Listening is both a skill you need to nurture and a habit. Listening becomes normal, with practice. You might think you're a good listener already. If so, this problem may not need to be sorted out. But consider asking certain people if they think you could improve your listening skills before you make that decision. Do try to avoid being defensive if they say yes!

*Giving compliments*

Giving compliments not only makes you feel better but also raises your self-confidence. When people respond positively to your efforts, you will gain confidence. Consider it a priority to offer at least two best wishes each day. It is believed this role will be rewarding and beneficial to you. When giving compliments follow these guidelines: be precise. Don't make grand, global statements like, "You're the world's best person," because most people will not believe you. On the opposite, consider something simpler and more specific like, "I loved the way you treated that sales meeting," or "This dinner is great." Don't pour with the positive into negative things. For example, don't say, "I loved the way you handled that sales meeting, particularly after the awful job you did last week," or "It's delicious this dinner. I wish you could cook like this every night. "If you haven't given any compliments in a while, then at first other people might react strangely. They might wonder what you're up to, and maybe even become a bit sarcastic. It is recommended that you continue to try, though. They will get used to the new you over time, and they'll probably respond to the change quite well.

*Pillowing rather than pillorying*

People with BPD often experience difficulties in getting other people to meet their needs. They complain that others don't hear them, or they don't feel comfortable asking for what they want directly. There is a strategy that can make it a little easier to get your needs met. This technique is called pillowing — rather than pillorying. You dish out abuse, contempt, and ridicule when pillorizing someone. How likely are other people to listen to you and do whatever you want while pillorying? Not very much.

However, you soften the blow as much as you can with pillowing whilst still clearly stating what you want. Pillowing can be done using some simple sentences. Such phrases will help you find out that you are not the world's one and only proprietor of truth and knowledge. That is to say; they help you understand that your point of view may be somewhat flawed. And, in fact, it's always — for everybody, whether they have BPD or not.

Here are some sample statements which can help you learn the technique of pillowing. They can be very helpful as you try to fill in other people's needs or demands. The pillowing phrase is in boldface:

I might be off base somehow, but I wondered if what you were saying was meant to hurt me?

Maybe I'm overly sensitive, but when you use that tone of voice, I can't hear you.

I know this might be an irritating question, but I feel so overwhelmed; do you mind taking over for a while?

I might be mistaken somehow, but it sounds like you're angry with me.

You don't want to use pillowing excessively, because if you do, others will find it somewhat unnatural. But the approach does make it easier to communicate your needs. Statements such as the ones above also help you feel as though you are less demanding of people. In fact, the approach makes listening to you an easier task for other people to perform.

# CONCLUSION

Until recently, many professionals had been convinced that a bit of consistency in their lives was the only achievable goal for BPD patients. The treatment outlined in this book seems to have far better results than an easy, stable life. However, people with borderline personality disorder (BPD) often become extremely emotional and may respond with great big emotions to minor stressors such as waiting in line at a grocery store, being stuck in a traffic jam, or hearing negative feedback. BPD psychotherapies help patients to control negative emotions by teaching them skills.

It is important to remember that many of BPD's symptoms are symptoms that everybody occasionally experiences. Additionally, some of the BPD symptoms overlap with other mental and physical conditions. BPD can be diagnosed only by a licensed professional.

The good news is that there is hope once a diagnosis has been made. The therapist or doctor may help determine an action plan which may include psychotherapy, medication, or other therapy. Research has shown that symptoms of BPD can be significantly reduced with good, consistent treatment. Some people who were once diagnosed with BPD no longer meet treatment and time criteria for the disorder.

CPSIA information can be obtained
at www.ICGtesting.com
Printed in the USA
LVHW051203060322
712743LV00001B/23

9 781803 035017